HISTORICAL FASHION COLORING BOOK

ELEGANT DRESSES OF THE 18TH CENTURY

ROCOCO, GEORGIAN,

MARIE ANTOINETTE,

AND FRENCH

REVOLUTION ERAS

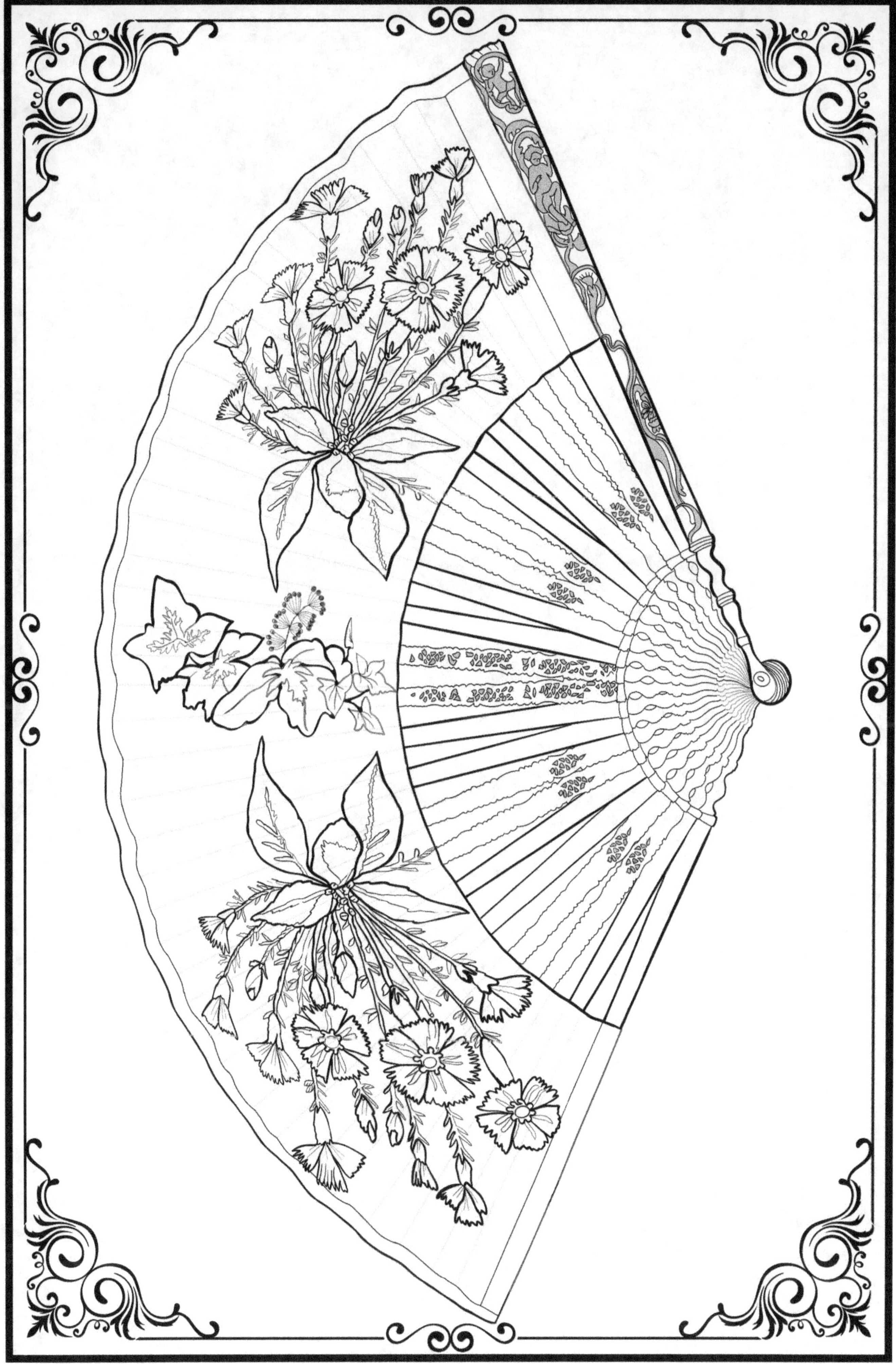

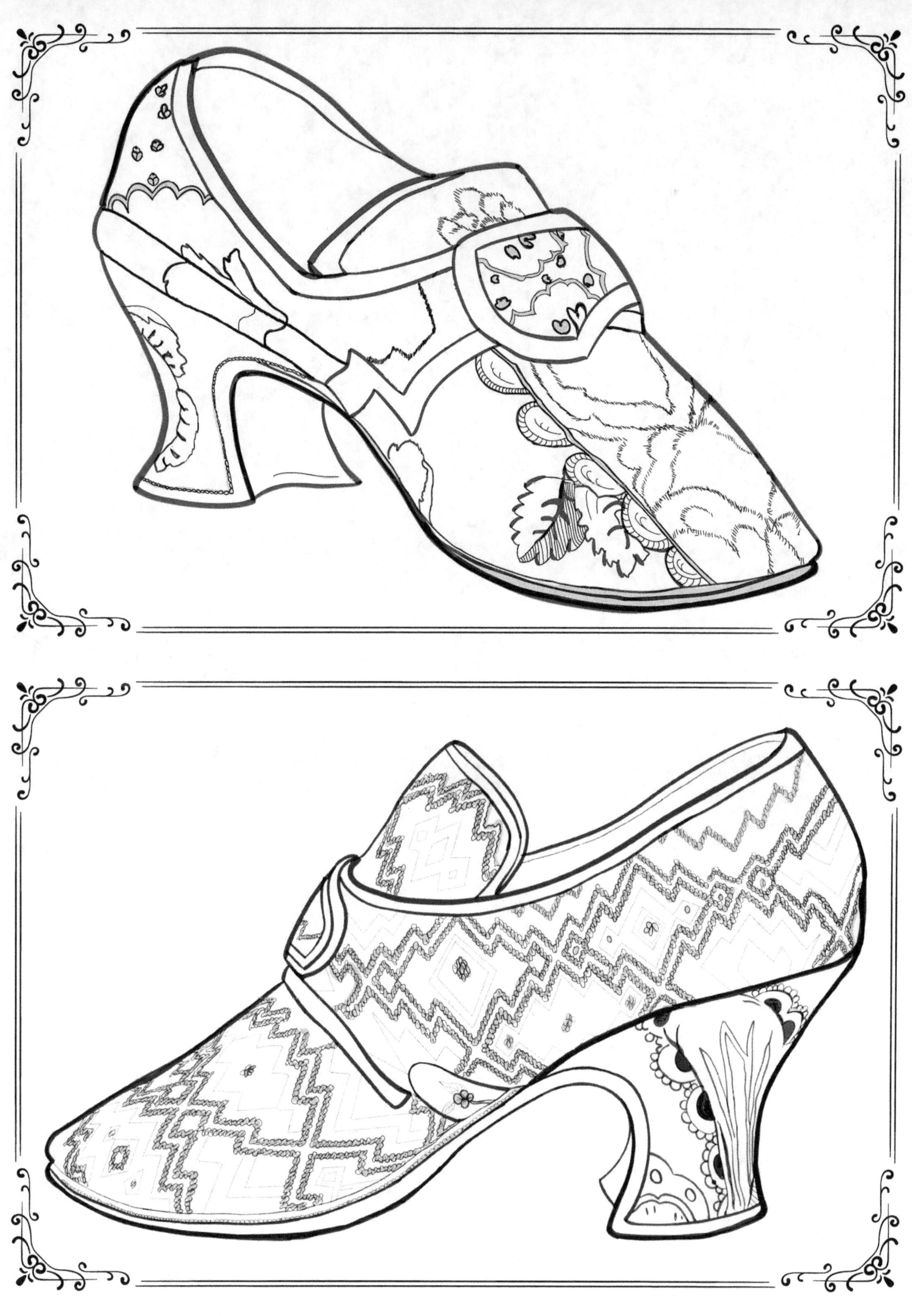

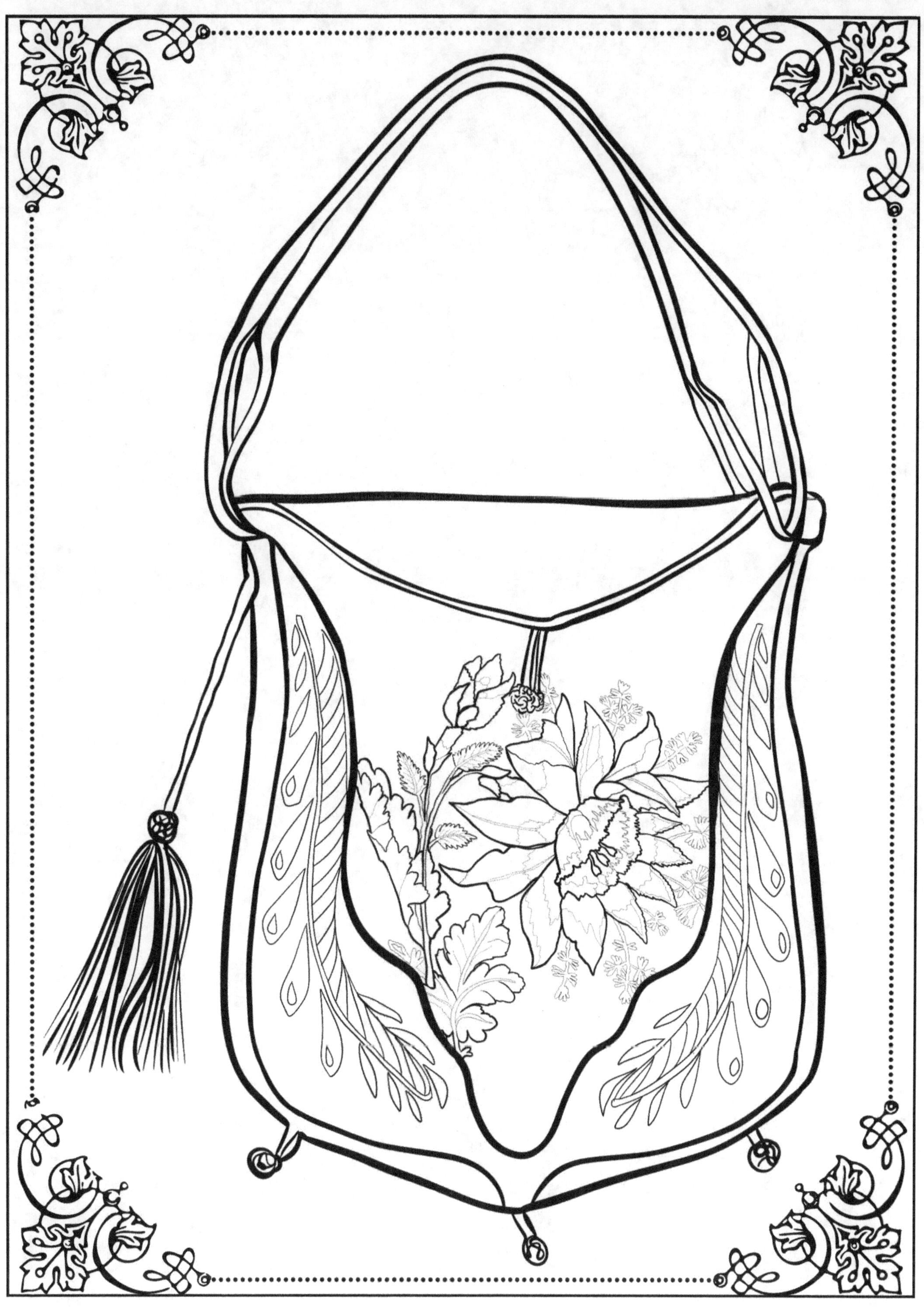

Thank You for Your Purchase!

I sincerely hope you enjoy bringing
the beautiful dresses of the 18th century to life
with your colors. This coloring book is a journey
through the exquisite fashion history of an
elegant era, and I am thrilled to share it with you.
Your support means the world to me,
and I am grateful that you've chosen
to explore this creative adventure.

Happy coloring!

TYPES OF 18TH-CENTURY DRESSES
TIMELINE

Mantua
c. 1700–1710

Dresses with panier
c. 1720

Robe volante
c. 1720–1730

Dress with quilted petticoat, c. 1730–40

Court dress
c. 1760

Robe à l'anglaise
c. 1750

Dress with wide panniers
c. 1750

Rococo fashion
c. 1760

Robe à la française
c. 1760–70

Robe à la française (sack back dress)
c. 1760–70

Court dress (grande robe de court)
c. 1775

Robe à la polonaise
c. 1775–85

Caraco (right)
c. 1775–1780

Redingote dress
c. 1780–1790

Dress from the French Revolution period, c. 1795

Robe à l'anglaise
c. 1780–90

Robe en chemise, (chemise à la reine- -Marie Antoinette)
c. 1780–1785

English court dress
c. 1798

Neoclassical, high-waisted dress
c. 1799

Empire dress
c. 1800